BABY SCHEMA

Isabel Galleymore's first collection, *Significant Other*, won the John Pollard Foundation International Poetry Prize in 2020 and was shortlisted for the Forward Best First Collection Prize and Seamus Heaney First Collection Prize. She held the position of Walter Jackson Bate Fellow at Harvard's Radcliffe Institute for Advanced Study in 2022-23. She lectures at the University of Birmingham.

Baby Schema
Isabel Galleymore

CARCANET POETRY

First published in Great Britain in 2024 by
Carcanet
Alliance House, 30 Cross Street
Manchester, M 2 7 A Q
www.carcanet.co.uk

A CIP catalogue record for this book is
available from the British Library.

ISBN 978 1 80017 388 0

Book design by Andrew Latimer, Carcanet
Typesetting by LiteBook Prepress Services
Printed in Great Britain by SRP Ltd, Exeter, Devon

The publisher acknowledges financial
assistance from Arts Council England.

CONTENTS

Forever, It Appears   11
Campaign   12
Busy, Busy   13
Head over Heels   14
My Earliest Memory   15
Coming Home   16
Night Thought   17
Squeezamal™   18
It's a Set Up   19
Fable   20
Mothers   21
Like Nothing Else   22
No Word   23
Morning   24
The Pitch   25
Good-Natured   26
Heritage   27
Because   28
Kidding   29
A Ha-Ha   30
Animal Product   31
So Adorable   32
Made You Look   33
On Earth   34
Disneyland   35
Friends   45
Career of Violence   46
Mammal Club   48
Baby Schema   49
Starting today   50
What Happened   51

This tree frog is going extinct   52
Uninvited   53
Interior Design   54
Algorithm   55
Release   56
No Show   57
...   58
Belonging   59
Lonesome George   60
Yellow Diamond   61
More and more   62
Little Fly   63
Madam   64
Semi-Unintelligible   65
Chosen   66
Outbound   67
Bird Watching   68

Notes   71
Acknowledgements   72

'The cute always in some sense designates a commodity in search of its mother'

— Lori Merish

'We may call them, if the terms are thought dignified enough, babble and doodle'

— Northrop Frye

BABY SCHEMA

FOREVER, IT APPEARS

I wake and find it's day again.
It happens every time.
It makes no difference if I crush
the day between my hands

or wring or drop, or squish the day
as if it were the frog –
the frog bath sponge instinctively
returns to its set shape –

I watch its simple eyes, so soft,
reopening like hours –
forever, it appears, expecting
to be taken care of.

When Aw succeeded Ah, Aw preached the importance of a pebble's freckled onesie, ignoring the mountain and its storm. Where Ah had ah'd over the ocean, Aw now aw'd over the ocean-dawdling dawn-hued prawn. With Ah far gone, attention turned towards the two-week seedlings of a lawn; a buzzard-hunted yawn-paused lizard; one carrot awfully small. How big the world became as it possessed once more the petit-four of insect eggs, a chicken's moon-clipped claws.

BUSY, BUSY

Don't you just love it when you're held up
by a slug? On the path,
this hunkling of fudge
is plugging away at the task
                of moving herself,
    a little feather
stuck to her side as if
she plans to hand herself over
to all that stuff ungummed from
        earth –
           don't you just love it?
        Don't you just
    love – ?

HEAD OVER HEELS

You tell me 'forever' will take too long
to add; your initials finished, mine just starting
into the trunk. We both know summer
is coming to a close in this park with small petting
zoo, a stray picnic blanket or two; the warden
pretty much out of sight – I check, check once more,
and watch as a wasp sheepdogs a huddle of children
across the grassy stretch. Smaller than the others,
one child remains beside the pen where the
Fainting Goat is kept; the animal continues to
observe its name every time the child tries
a shriek or scream. Again, again. It's difficult to say
which the child loves best: the goat, or its four legs
swivelling up to the sky. One day I'll know
that this was the most romantic way
to tell me you carried a knife.

MY EARLIEST MEMORY

is looking from the cave and
thinking the forest stupid
because it would let me do to it
anything I wanted – bees were beginning to potter
around a manifesto manifested in blooms
and little grasses of what
was promised freely – prairie,
mountain, ocean – to I and the every-
bodies of avian maximums, bughoods, tacky
amphibians, I was expected to permit
love, claw, peace, nip-
me-to-pieces species, pleated cacti, even
small waters afrenzy with larvae-like paisleys half dreaming
of making me sick – what was financing this
radical experiment growing rapidly
eccentric with oversharings of clown
and cat-clothed fish, for which
I had a soft spot, for which
I had no use, like the swamp I'd once played in, long ago
grown out of – what can I say –
I wanted nothing to do with it and now
from where I speak to you,
each beak-preachy dawn coming quickly undone,
I wait not knowing what
the next big vision is
and already I am firmly behind it.

COMING HOME

Catkins kittenish on the alpine breeze.
She's climbing in the dawn
of the twentieth century. When she falls
she is expertly preserved;
the glacier keeps her filed
beneath skies in which planes will advance
to carry TVs, me watching a film
greasy with romance and apocalypse
because on some level I revel
in the thought of being properly fucked.
What is our estimated arrival?
I eat my handful of pretzels high above
the ice relaxing all over the mountain;
her head like a nipple just surfacing.

NIGHT THOUGHT

Around the time we were meant
to save the earth, I failed
to send a picture of my houseplant
in flower to a friend –

my attachment, I was warned, too large,
but soon the leaves grew dull;
how dare the plant waste all my love,
I thought, and locked it out –

a bad dog – in the yard.
Later, restive with the lack of give
in my pyjamas, I wondered if
I should go barefoot and save

what I'd left outdoors,
but beyond the bed was cold
and I uncertain as to whether
it deserved me anymore.

SQUEEZAMAL™

I'd left the house, citing a walk.
6pm, a few degrees above freezing.
On somebody's dashboard,
a soft toy; lilac-furred and
smiling. Baby
monkey-esque. A breast measure
of squishiness. It possessed
an explicitly-loving gaze
I might've judged mildly obscene,
but that evening I needed to find the soft
toy benign. The soft
toy was eager to love me.
And it did so, I felt,
comprehensively. In that moment
on the street, a stranger passed
between us
and I saw how its moon-eyed look
remained, adoring him
just as much as me, presumably
capable of adoring wholesale:
it was so indiscriminate
in its loving, I couldn't help feeling angry,
disappointed in myself.

IT'S A SET UP

Mind hurtles into the field, brushes
a stem-
tipped snail
who's lost all track of time,
I like to think, forgetting I shouldn't
make an impression – do I
agonise or
leap – I being the hero
who discovers the floor is rigged
with a delicate trip-wire
system – grasses,
insects, dewy blooms of
moss and shrubby flower – by such
abundant hurtability, I find myself
surrounded.

FABLE

Trees crawling with babies, babies
darting through the sky
or buoyed by thermal vents, babies
painted with false eyes

repelling bad-boy babies, babies
grazing, babies grizzly,
under a plant pot, a medley of babies
in outfits tidily slimy,

babies nesting in other babies
of cliff and reef and briar,
growing, owing to our negligence,
ever babier.

MOTHERS

As we watch our friend's toddler push
a pram with her own little baby inside
you ask me, *Did you ever have one?*

Yes, I say, thinking back to the doll
to which (to whom?) I never gave a name
and – because I lost her clothes

or gave them to my bears –
was permanently nude. I don't know why
I often liked to go outside and send

her synthetic-resin body flying
onto the shed roof, and then
beg my mother to retrieve her

so I could do it again. *Where is she now?*
you enquire as if she might be nestled
in boxes we keep under the stairs

but I don't have her
and haven't for a while – assume she was
thrown out, before I remember

there's no such thing as throwing out
and she is, will be for years, somewhere.

LIKE NOTHING ELSE

Why would you have a child, the toad
in the wet grass asks,
the earwig asks
as you carry each away from where you dig –
it's something to do
with love, you're meant to
say, remembering what
you've heard of the devotion
coming soon as they're born;
like nothing else
in the world
exists
and who are you then, where is

the toad, the earwig – not in sight – already
you're looking at your watch, the droopy-
teated fuchsia you'd planned to
plant, and now in the shadow of
your foot – a woodlouse:
do you see it –
a tiny telephone –
will this still exist, will you
lift it to your ear, and if so, then what –
a crackle
of fourteen moving legs, as it should be
perhaps, the line no
longer any good.

NO WORD

If I draw a mouth on an apple, does it
possess more or less opportunity
to speak? If I find a rare bee orchid
in the grass, can I call this plant,
as I see this plant, a sex doll for the bee?
Bullfinch in the buckthorn above me.
I ask the bird to talk. No word
until a sing-song voice begins: *Isabel*
says a bird like me would say … and I –
I turn away. Rain is due. It's an hour
back to the road, back past the hills
stickered with sheep, a single cow –
her name printed across her body
in black and white – unreadably big.

MORNING

I see a person – hi – I say,
and to their dog – well, howdy pal
oh petal, babe and aren't you just –
and to the person – hey.

Standing behind and ahead:
the minute and its siblings.
All is possible in the future, I hear,
including the future's ending.

And when I see the dog, I say
a ha ha ha and oh my gosh
does someone want a smooch –
and to the person – morning –

THE PITCH

Because rhinos haven't adopted the small
muscle responsible for puppy dog eyes,
the species goes bankrupt.
Its regional stores close down.
How are we to survive this difficult climate

of you being so very uninterested in me?
When you turn away in bed,
all I can do is baby the pitch
of my voice. The body's an amazing
thing. Instinctively rebranding itself

to keep, if not increase, your investment
the bear became a toy bear, later
a cartoon of the toy. It's key to discover
a need nobody knows that they have.
In the dark, I tug on your sleeve.

GOOD-NATURED

You've felt hungry, unlooked-after of late.
You've walked, uncertain where to go, and now
you sit on this front step in first light

where a rosebush self-congratulates
and a sign – LOST CAT – sticks in the window.
You've felt hungry, unlooked-after of late

and the cat is your stock cat: tabby-striped,
though these days probably a bit uncombed.
Sitting on this front step in first light

as starlings glitch above, you might
wonder if the cat's name is actually your own;
you've felt so hungry, unlooked-after of late.
You wait on this front step in first light.

HERITAGE

Like a glossy nativity scene;
the barrels of pansies, the swept platform,
the canopy's preserved supports
being repainted by a man in vintage overalls
and we are talking about where to go

for dinner when in it comes –
smoking like a cartoon baddie,
but we are also talking about the days
ahead, your job, and the station master
checks the time twice, and you should

leave the company and where
could we live? Tickets punched,
fields open before us – tired
from the outstanding summer
again, we are talking about the mortgage

and what we can set aside
while the *choo choo* scatters some birds,
which from here look vintage
too, small, so pretty and children,
what could we offer them.

BECAUSE

We knew we had to wait until we found a good
reason to have one. We'd heard about the farmer couple
who sought to expand into peas and beans
and so had one (and later another) as did the family
soap manufacturer that required more hands
to release the soaps from their casts, which gave
the impression the soaps were MADE WITH LOVING
CARE, to meet growing demand.
Understanding children to be the future
who would go on to fix several of the world's most
pressing problems, some people, including our neighbours,
had one. It lay like a sandbag in its mother's arms.
Occasionally I'd sigh, *I just want one!*
We need a good reason, you'd reply without hesitation.
Like this, quietly, a few years came and went.
Then, one spring in which every dawn came
pigletty and the blossom trees were really putting in
the work, I dropped an earring into the gap
of the living room floorboards that only a small hand
could retrieve, and I gave you the look
and you carried me up the stairs.

KIDDING

It was relatively swift
to make a life today
while looking from the window at
the logo of a cleaning company:
a duckling
lemon-yellow, seeming happy-free,

and lives just getting going
were making lives themselves
in the crèche across the road –
from dough came eggs and snakes,
a dolly did a chore,
a flower sang – and would she be

like or not like me. I imagined her
waddling routine as a fruit-fly landed
ding-dong on my skin
and before I thought to say
hello
I'd already smudged the thing.

A HA-HA

At first, they think I am a tree
and, as such, a hug repository
and then they think no, not tree,
but where it grows – a grand estate –
the love I offer is a listed structure
and its generous prospect in which
gardens and grounds look unabridged

when between them a ha-ha is –
how could they have known – my love
was built to stop the livestock
clopping in and sitting at the escritoire
or hoofing at the cookie jar –
my love was built to stop.

ANIMAL PRODUCT

When my father falls and bruises
his vestigial tail,
or when a catcall fills the street
or when, without a thought, I eat

a little pig comprised of pig
from a bag of sweets,
or when, in the leathery night,
goosebumps hatch across

my skin, instinctively again
my daughter nuzzles for my breast,
which I muzzle by my not
having had her yet, or when

SO ADORABLE

The kittens are so adorable I could die!
The potato with a deep cut like a dolphin smile
a little less so – still, at the market,
I consider taking it home. These days
everything tells me: submit to love.

The kittens are so adorable I could die!
And if I don't, or can't? No doubt
this would reflect badly on me. I confide
to a friend who's already made a list
of beneficiaries, understanding

the kittens are so adorable, I could die!
I begin to eat and sleep as though
for the last time. Waking, at my window
I find the wet nose of a leaf. I hold
my body tight, which is, for now, all mine.

MADE YOU LOOK

That afternoon, as I walked, a girl
approached, warned me my shoelace was undone
    and as I looked down at my pull-on, intrinsically
    shoelaceless-boots, laughter
from the girl and her friends spilled out. A breeze
had begun and, across the street,
    a horse chestnut's arrows of blossom
    were pointing in every direction. Had the girl
pretended to care for me? Was the joke me
convinced by her phony concern,
    believing I'd trip, fall? I'd accepted her caution
    when the caution hadn't been
necessary. I like remembering it –
the afternoon; the soft arrows, the girls –
    merry – laughing, some laughing so hard because
    I was so far from harm.

ON EARTH

Wow, the nature living here,
the plant that, wow, blooms in circles
and wow, the shadows of each petal,
wow, the natter neverminded,

wow, the newt's stare in amongst
the complex nounshire living here,
nowhere, wow, the nose hair, wild,
abundant gnome-ware living here,

wow, the beetroot's ratty tail,
terry towel-like lichen, also wow,
shhh I say, these wows too much,
but what on earth am I to do;
beneath this sky dolloped with cloud
every breath is made of wow.

DISNEYLAND

Making eye-contact with a squirrel
for a second or three too long,
I find myself still waiting
for nature to wave back.

Here you can really get up close.
A chipmunk knees a toddler over.
It's a delicatessen of animism
and its shopkeeper is a mouse.

He flings out his arms in welcome.

              Michael –
whistling dreamster,
              Michael mouse –
minstrel-gloved, four-fingered,
no nursery of mites in your fur, here

air is textured with glockenspiel and popcorn,
not a leaf is out of place,
one boy uttery with *momie*
anticipating his 12pm MEET AND GREET with a lion.

That they're capable of love, no one can be certain.

Mothers in this particular landscape are,
by tradition, evil or absent
and with my absent child, I sit in the shade of a castle
built in kind of, decorated in quite.

Close by, a sparrow (very small)
behaves as if this place is real (it's not
not) and knocks her beak against (I watch)
a Thai-green curry crisp on the cobbled floor.

Several feathers are like a wave washed up untidily white
on her side, her flax-seed eye – unblinking, aloof –
and all the time I notice this, a fly
rests on my breast like my breast's a piece of fruit
in a seventeenth-century, Dutch still life.

Alongside pops of wild
west gunshots, a blown
kiss from a princess floats
above a duck who's nude
below the waist, the kiss
drifts up and over
EDISON AVENUE, rococo
scroll, cheshire cat and
caterpillar, the labyrinth
grown from yew in which
the dodo's lost; dressed
in a damson overcoat,
he's saying *which way?*
which way? Pipe in hand,
he'll be lost forever, but
extraordinarily good-
humoured

(and – where – with all these
boundaries crossed – am I? –
adjusting – and also – my ponytail –
who?)

BILLY
BOB'S MAC N CHEESE   ARABIAN TREASURE

piles of
looking – salty –
        what is she doing
        with a notebook open – am I
        something funny
not wearing you – your ears – omnipresent, always
        unhearing – you

                Michael of the Wrist Tattoo
                Michael of the Waffle
                Michael of the Band Aid pressed
                against a Blistered Ankle

am I

a part	of the family	happy,	off-sprung
loner	loping	through	the afternoon
that	chatters	about its	record temperature
wonders	at the what	ever after	while
a reduced	population	of animals	labour

In cherry tulle and booties,
minuscule dictators coca-cola to
an off-grid, sylvan rhythm.
With a breeze, screams leak
from the neighbouring theme;
each rose is a nodding dog.

Long ago, gun-slinging and snouted, Michael found joy in playing music with the bodies of his friends. The highest notes he prodded from a piglet's tender spots. Now, rehabilitated, love's played on loop and no child is eaten by an alligator, no employee's electrocuted at Phantom Manor because here it's not permissible for death to be pronounced.

Don't we queue for the day
in our sleep,

and the day comes round like a pleasure
                buggy –
        aren't we babies

pushed through each dioramic scene?
        The way my cat's blood travels (jerky and erratic)
in the black cab of a flea

we enter pastures painted in jades and kermits
        (inhabited by faces (their eyeballs
    possessing no looking of their own)) before a fit

of movement into storms;
            one poorly-lit mid-century moral,
some life-eventful turn.

Later, I'll realise I was happiest at the detail
                    of the animatronic boar
               whose wiring made his
styrene muscle
                    twitch in one leg and nothing
   more –
                         wired, only, to do a
   dream
                    beneath a patch of yellow-
                    splendored gorse

where gorse once really grew. Here, weren't there fields for miles to
see? Plugged with beetroot and beetroot's fountain of waxy leaves?
Its flower – a tiny spatchcocked chicken? And
weeds; dandelions,

thistles at least, and aphids,
hoverflies, lanky-looking ants,
earwigs, horse shit, bees. A
bumbling movement cues my
attention to what must be
a human cling-filmed in sweat,
cling-filmed in sweat inside
the costume of a cricket;
a cricket dressed like a fat-cat
banker in top hat, who returns
the gaze of a little girl (distantly,
fire plays the part of fire
in a choreographed disaster)
and waves.

FRIENDS

The insects are going into storage.
Does the museum
rent the same place, just
out of town,

where my friends took
their furniture before
going abroad? And what for?
A new extinction

display – animals admirable,
unfoldable, ready
whenever they choose to return
and set up home properly.

CAREER OF VIOLENCE

Didn't I pick at and bruise
the garden you grew?
I wrote my name, drew my face
in every one of your books, set the woods
aflame and then
the prairie, like I hated you, which
to some degree was true, and constantly
I'd tug on your arm
as if it were an awfully stretched teat
for what you couldn't afford to give me and
gave me – one afternoon, a monkey,
bird, bear and, one by one, I dropped
them from existence, but –
wasn't it you who picked them up
from the floor
and returned each to me
in my highchair, good
as new – and all of this without
reprove? – you,
who never said no, never
set down rules, who allows me,
even now, to speak over you?

And now you're up and leaving,
taking with you all the good
scenery, weather quickly
turning family-
unfriendly – why? Don't
you know once you're gone,
you give me no chance
to show you how good I can be?

MAMMAL CLUB

When I find a lump like a marble;
a choking hazard in one of my body's sippy cups,
   yes, those parts of myself
   permitting me entrance to the mammal club,
I'm reminded that special rank exists
for animals who breastfeed their young;
   that this is a fact like I breathe
   every other breath because of plankton;
plankton, which is too small for the human
eye to perceive, has breathfed me
   since my conception. It's nothing,
   the specialist tells me, this requires
no further attention, and I breathe
another breath because of plankton;
   plankton, too small for the human
   to believe could be a mamma.

BABY SCHEMA

I like the word *mother* only
because I'm still a child – or want
to be – the one cared for; no debt,
nothing on file. To shrug

off adulthood the way the statue
on the street has let his stone head
wear away to a chubby-cheeked,
big-eyed roundedness that stares

bemused? Perhaps concerned?
How I stare when I see
the child next door
who drags a watering can between
wilting shrubs
like a child and not at all.

you could be a daddy to the arts,
       and also bring home a symphony.
Can I adopt a donkey? And a picnic bench, a dodo
bone named Charlie who needs

a dehumidifier to keep
       him inside the museum even more
comfortably. Can I matron an ecosystem? One can
become a good parent

company for a non-bio soap
       subsidiary, get busy making
some family from a stranger's vocabulary, why not
god a magnolia into adolescently-fuzzy bud.

WHAT HAPPENED

As if to make a point about its helplessness,
the animal grew smaller each day
until shortly it seemed to loom over us
and so, diligent as always, we
added the animal's name to the list.

Birds rehearsed their jingles, magnolias re-released
their fists of middle fingers,
years came easy as breath and no,
we didn't hear the phone –
one of us in the garden, one of us at the shops –

the animal picked up the call:
apparently, an opening had become available –
one of us sipping tea, one of us checking the hour,
the minute – and the animal, small, smallest by now,
dropped straight into it.

and so you should prepare yourself for sadness. This is what they told the woman. 'What kind of sadness?', the woman asked, but they had already closed the door: she and the last of the species were to have exactly three minutes together. On a small square of moss, the tree frog sat stillish as if it were a jelly doorstop. Each of its eyes stared like a Magic 8 Ball. She picked up the frog. Already one minute had passed. 'Is it a *crying* kind of sadness?', she asked, directing the question to the amphibian. 'Most Likely', one eye responded. The other eye: 'Concentrate & Ask Again'. There had been a time when the Magic 8 Ball was easy to spot; in people's homes, all manner of shops. Now, she realised, she hadn't seen one in years. From somewhere in the room, a croak-croak alarm began to sound, which seemed, even to her, insensitively chosen. The frog shut down its eyes. The woman thought about shaking it gently for an answer to a question she would formulate later, but it was time to go. 'I'm sorry for your loss', she said so quietly she could have been talking to herself.

UNINVITED

Turning my (uninvited)
attention to the fuchsia (weeding out
the rest of the garden) I observe

(neither her colour, nor what kind
of day she's having) only
her pollen feet in tiny slippers
stitched from faux fur

and kicking out towards me
in the wind. Is inattention
tenderer? Should I

put myself away from earth,
stem and bud, like one who
(with hands cupped) relocates
a spider from the house.

INTERIOR DESIGN

Bringing them home for the first time
I wondered, had I made the right
choice, but
already I was a year or
two down the line, wiping, from their faces,
soft landscapes
of porridge – too late
to return them – what a joke, and anyway
they'd begun
to seem sort of
special; not just to me,
but also to you and our friends who extended
compliments when they stopped by
for lunch, and
the more I thought about it, the more I
knew the choice hadn't really
been a choice at all – having them
was the way
of carrying on; otherwise in what wildness
would I live? Here
I am, then, at the end of the day, washing,
toweling them dry,
not so much for their sake
as mine.

ALGORITHM

The bowl has three pet peanuts —
each one a peanut plant's attempt
to outlive itself. My phone lights up

like it's my mind with the thought
of having a child. It suggests I watch
This Lovable Otter Will Get You Through.

The day is long, weather too much,
but no more than we were told to expect.
The bowl has three pet peanuts —

each one a peanut plant's attempt
to outlive itself. Should I repeat myself?
How else to ride out time?

When This Lovable Otter
comes to an end
I play it again.

RELEASE

That night, when I got home, I learnt
a tree frog species had been lost
and my body was releasing its usual sum of blood.
I only had a few years left, my mother
often warned, and I watched

footage of the tree frog sitting about
in its tank, the clip of the frog's 'lonely' call.
Was I angry or sorry? Whichever.
This couldn't be called a crisis. It happened
every month, and I went on

reading about the breeding programmes,
the experts' relentless watching of the frog
and, as if the amphibian was an unresponsive
photocopier, their frustration, their
tinkering, the time they spent waiting

the way my mother waited, and who could say
whether I felt regret or happiness
when the tender muscle cramped and spasmed
and the tree frog made its leap away –
lost, they said, or maybe free.

NO SHOW

In the rhododendron's shadow,
Alejandro dropped his
rainbow-glittered dodo.
Cheerio the robin calls, *yolo*
calls the dodo. From the
pigeon's genome comes a
unicornucopia of dodoistic
echoes and dunnos. A woman
cries out *Dodo?* for her
far-fetching fido lost-looking
on the slip road. Two-starry
and a stone's throw from
Piazza del Duomo, you'll find
the Casa Dodo (with an etching
of a dodo hanging solo
from the dado) permanently
closed.

...

apropos these end times, what use for the
        lyric? Each
version of this question I hunger to answer:
        I made a idea but
I eated it!! My soul enrolled

in internet loldom perceives certain
        benefits
of quietly quitting like the soil beneath the
        sorghum does. Envying
each and every dot dot dot

between reported thought and action,
        sometimes I
long to be one end-of-summer dandelion
        dressed dumb or delphic with
its exquisitely airy head

BELONGING

I don't remember
this snout, this washable stink,
but I held him all through the night
like a regular nature lover.

Does the bear possess knowledge
of me in his unmuscly memory?
His tiredness suggests
he was my everything –

and I to him? And still?
Only lately, his outdoorsiness
was evolved to have more give
and give more love – and it was felt

that when it fell from our clutch
our furred and pawed belonging
should fall softly-stuffed so as
to never wake us up.

LONESOME GEORGE

A good nursery was prepared for George in 1919, Chicago, Illinois.
George who'd later become a semi-successful country musician
and the comedian of his day,
  also a tortoise.
  This wrinkled, helpless being
  delivered by the researchers in 1971
  from one island of the Galapagos
  to another, christening him George
because of George's amusingly-lonely monologues on TV.
One of a kind, newspapers announced – and fan after fan
desperate to see him live on stage
  wanting to be able to say they had seen
  his crawl – slow and primordial,
  his grandfatherly face lifting
  on that neck. His shell
  like a giant's toenail,
before heart trouble at 71; survived by his wife, Alice
and their three children,
  before his heart grew weak
  aged 80 (they guessed)
  and taking the species with him,
George fell fast asleep.

YELLOW DIAMOND

SLOW and YIELD the signs kept on
being ignored as we sped past
the city rich in hate appeal.
Downhill, outskirted were trees
loud with Pollinate Me Now

Or I Will Bear No Fruit!
The month too hot. Some animals
turning into full stops. Was this
a suitable moment to overtake?
A yellow diamond of anxiety

looked firmly back at me.
I needed to be careful: up ahead
there was a baby on board.
By continuing to exist, we each
recede from preciousness.

MORE AND MORE

I picture him: a sticky-fingered, pint-sized
version of myself toddling through the aisles
where items are stacked high;
a moth-eaten koala beneath a ringtail possum,
a series of glass-eyed macaws and
in this moment I'm stroking his hair,
using the same endearment my mother used
for me – *darling* – before my hand strokes air
and he's zooming away – *nee-naw nee-naw* –
little spirit medium of emergency vehicles;
the sound ricocheting between the displays
of bear upon bear, the plain and striped cats,
while a crayon falls from his dungarees –
from a pocket that he always, as if by instinct,
overstuffs, and pausing to retrieve what's lost,
I hasten to catch him up, where
the shelves are emptier now – a few bottled
reptiles, the squat skeleton of something
I see his hand reaching out towards
and the world better off without him.

LITTLE FLY

Because the thought was very bad
and unerasable
I told myself the thought
was little as a fly,

littler still as I perceived
the fly on tippy toes,
a dimple in the air I'd watch
boop against my window –

oh hello cupcake, sugar pot,
I'd say to my winged thought,
or it would say to me, latched on,
oh I could eat you up.

MADAM

Beneath the jaws of bunting, didn't
my friends present their newborn –

and didn't we cluster around her
like the fresh meat that she was –

my body and I, we wondered
wasn't it similar to sky-diving –

shouldn't I do or have done
the experience – of motherhood

wasn't I browsing – the shop floor
shapely with pink/blue balloons –

and didn't I greet my reflection
How can I help you today –

is it yourself or your would-be baby
Madam's looking to consume?

SEMI-UNINTELLIGIBLE

Restless with deserving, I'd bought myself
a kitten. Semi-unintelligible,
she was primed for fable. I could caption
her with anything. Though mostly what
I wanted was to dress her as a lion.

If you like this, then you'll like that
ads frequently addressed me. And
I knew it to be true. My lungs
forever doting on this specific breath,
only to swiftly discard it for the next,

the next. What did I desire exactly?
I had no answer to the question
whether the costume would make her
more animal or more human.

CHOSEN

Are you a you? No right
to personhood – mostly
imagined by me, midnightly,
on account of your scratching
in the wall – companionable.
Also I wish you'd go, but then
some say you come with
the territory;
      being a woman
I know women who have you
(even a few) inside the house,
named and dressed in miniature
pantaloons, which makes me wonder
if the scratching's not in fact
knocking: you
      wanting to come in
(like them) and sweetly
burgle my life. I shouldn't
presume. This inbetweenness
you inhabit – why couldn't
it be the place that you've
chosen; the place I can trust
you are happiest?

OUTBOUND

In the hot morning air, we're waiting for it –
     you, I, the man who's failing to end a call
bye, take care, ok, you too, perhaps out of
     awkwardness or love. One two-year old
chews on a rhino. Her twin squeezes shut
     her eyes. Terrified once, weren't we –
of the engine, of ourselves accelerating
     over earth; would we be able to breathe,
people asked. Quickly, the child's attention
     turns from horn to hind leg. It's automatic –
the announcement – what's coming to take
     us away is on time. As if in reply, cricket
chitter and birdcry press into the pauses
     between his every *talk soon* and *bye bye.*

BIRD WATCHING

A surprise to find amid this year's
cohort of
leaves, a bird with its
back to me. What was the
bird watching
or was it staring into
space or into a thought
all its own? I went to say
ahem, but
it turned out
my mouth was gone.
A surprise.
The bird with its
back to me as if
I could be the background.

The term 'Baby Schema' originates from Konrad Lorenz's identification of 'Kindchenschema': a set of infantile physical features (such as large eyes and chubby cheeks) that convey vulnerability and trigger care-giving behaviour.

2023 marked 100 years of The Walt Disney Company. Each page of 'Disneyland' consists of 100 syllables. The sequence makes reference to both real and imagined signage in Disneyland Paris. Parts of the poem's form are influenced by Hope Mirrlees's 'Paris: A Poem'.

'This tree frog is going extinct' and 'Release' respond to the death of Toughie, the last known Rabbs' fringe-limbed tree frog, in 2016.

ACKNOWLEDGEMENTS

Thanks are due to the following publications in which these poems first appeared or were commissioned: *Poetry Review* ('Little Fly', 'Because'); *Magma* ('This tree frog is going extinct'); *The Times Literary Supplement* ('More and more'); *Poetry Birmingham Literary Journal* ('Animal Product', 'Squeezamal™'); *The New York Review of Books* ('Interior Design'); *The Drift* ('Semi-Unintelligible'); *Poetry* ('Forever, It Appears', 'Release'); *Oxford Poetry* ('The Pitch').

I am grateful to Gladstone's Library for hosting me as a Writer in Residence in 2021 and to the University of Birmingham for funding my research visit to Disneyland Paris. My sincere thanks to the staff and my fellow fellows at Harvard University's Radcliffe Institute for Advanced Study and to the Arts and Humanities Research Council, part of UK Research and Innovation.

My gratitude to Rowland Bagnall, Tara Bergin, Gabrielle Calvocoressi, Jenna Clake, Caroline Harris, Emily Hasler, Luke Kennard, Sharanya Murali, Andrés Triana Solórzano and beloved Zellig poets.

Especial thanks to Jorie Graham, John McAuliffe and Jazmine Linklater at Carcanet Press, Robert Peake, Declan Ryan and Phil Child – to whom this book is dedicated with love.